The Hunterian Museum Poems

The Hunterian Museum Poems

A History of the World in Objects and Poems

Edited by **Alan Riach**

First published in the UK, 2017

Freight Design
49-53 Virginia Street
Glasgow, G1 1TS
www.freightdesign.co.uk

A CIP catalogue reference for this book is available from the
British Library

ISBN 978-1-908754-78-3

Typeset by Freight in Berlingske
Printed & bound in Poland by Hussar Books.

Contents

FIVE: The Move
– Jemima Blackburn, *Moving the Contents of the Old College Museum*
Lesley Duncan, 'The Move from High Street to Gilmorehill (1870)'

SIX: Modernity
– Prosthetic hands
Jane Goldman, 'Andrew and the Hands'
– Model Newcomen steam engine
Jim Carruth, 'Spending Time with Model Newcomen Steam Engine'
– Death mask of Voltaire
John Glenday, 'On the Nature and Propagation of Fire'
– Diseased skull
Pàdraig MacAoidh/Peter Mackay, 'Spirochaete'
– Curling medal
Sheena Blackhall, 'The Curler's Coort'
– Sir Hubert von Herkomer, *Lord Kelvin*
Jim Carruth, 'Lord Kelvin's Second Law of Thermodynamics (1851)'
– Twin-headed deer
Gerry Cambridge, 'Untitled'
– Artificial pitch glacier
John Purser, 'GLAHM 113597'
– Chicken heads
Jim Carruth, 'Heads Up'
– Plaster cast of the gravid uterus
Richie McCaffery, 'Delivery'
– Ultrasound scanner
Peter McCarey, 'First Experimental Contact B-Scanner British Patent No.863.874'

SEVEN: The Hunterian Collection
– Allan Ramsay, *William Hunter*
Gerrie Fellows, 'The Curiosities of Dr Hunter'

The Hunterian Museum at the Old College, drawn by E. H. Shepherd, engraved by A. Fox, 1820-30

The Hunterian Museum

The first volume of poems produced from the collections of The Hunterian took our paintings and works of art as a starting point. The words in this little book all take a museum object as their point of departure: a natural history specimen, an archaeological artefact, one form or another of the material culture which represents human creativity and enquiry across several thousand years and several continents. As with the paintings previously selected by our wonderful poets, all the objects in the present volume have come to enter the collection of The Hunterian through a process of deliberate selection: they were singled out through various acts of careful and creative assembly and taxonomy with the recognition that they held the potential to stimulate intellectual enquiry and to communicate ideas, both individually and in juxtaposition.

The selection and arrangement of museum objects in a display case might appear to be closely analogous with the process of selecting and ordering words for prose or poetry. What the visitor encounters when entering the magnificent gothic halls of Sir George Gilbert Scott's Hunterian Museum (which will celebrate their 150th anniversary in 2020), is the very deliberate result of multiple processes of synthesis: the curatorial task of selecting and placing objects in carefully designed spaces, forming visually and intellectually modulated sequences intended to communicate meaning across an astonishing variety of materiality which happens to have arrived in the collection of the University of Glasgow over a period of some three centuries.

The processes of teaching and research which are at the core of a university's business have always generated 'stuff', whether the 'stuff' which gathers in research laboratories and teaching spaces and eventually becomes the 'stuff' of a formal museum, or the celebrated gifts and acquisitions which also come to a major collection. Even before William Hunter's astonishing bequest of 1783, which formally established The Hunterian, the University had been working with objects and accreting materials which are still on display to this day. As early as the mid-1760s, John Anderson, erstwhile Professor of Oriental Languages and subsequently Professor of Natural Philosophy, had suggested that the collections of the University should be constituted into an official museum. While Anderson's specific ambition remained unrealised, Gilbert Scott's museum was not the first building to house the University's collections, his gothic design a Victorian riposte to the chaste Georgian neoclassicism of William Stark's 1807 museum-temple, built amidst the 17th-century courtyards of the Old College on the High Street. Anderson's museum would have held teaching materials for Natural History and the scientific instruments used and maintained (by James Watt no less) within the University before themselves becoming historic artefacts and eventually part of the collection. Most remarkably of all, as 17th and 18th-century rural improvement and civil engineering projects had started to transform the central belt of Scotland, the astonishing archaeological material found along the line of the Antonine Wall was making its way into the only institution able to look after and interpret it, the University of Glasgow. These Roman collections, significantly predating the arrival of Hunter's bequest, themselves constituted both tourist attraction and material for research and practical instruction in the visual arts.

Hunter's astonishing bequest was housed in the museum building he endowed for little more than some sixty years before the University left Glasgow's High Street to move to Gilmorehill in 1870. Jemima Blackburn was on hand to record, in a wonderful watercolour, the contents of the museum on its way through the Glasgow streets. While Hunter's own Egyptian mummy, and much of his taxidermy collection failed to survive the vagaries of travel, display and two centuries of wear and tear, his anatomical preparations, casts and drawings, gathered in a lifetime's investigation of the Gravid Uterus, his library, including the great *Map of the Whole World* made in the late 17th century by a Jesuit missionary to the Chinese Imperial Court, and much of the material representation of the Enlightenment world of knowledge which he so assiduously assembled and preserved for its utility is still available for us to see.

To Hunter, as the first Professor of Anatomy at the Royal Academy in London, engagement with the practice of artists was a critical element in his recording and communicating scientific and medical knowledge. Stark's 1807 Hunterian building broke new ground in its design as a repository for the materials of both art and science, the 'two cultures' of which were diverging significantly even as Hunter's bequest finally reached Glasgow. It is easy to forget that it is Stark's Hunterian, not Gilbert Scott's which was first known to key figures associated with the practice of science in 19th-century Glasgow, most notably William Thomson, Lord Kelvin. While Kelvin's visually powerful teaching experiments, including the *Artificial Pitch Glacier*, are themselves entirely associated with Gilbert Scott's high Victorian Gothic buildings, his scientific achievements recognised with a knighthood in 1866 had all been developed while working in the Old College. Gilbert Scott's great museum building formed one wing of a complex housing the University's collections, the other containing the Library. Until the late 1970s Hunter's art collections, joined with great gifts and bequests such as those which constitute the Whistler Estate, were all shown together, Hunter's intentions extended into the 19th and 20th centuries.

If William Whitfield's 1970s Art Gallery separated the art collections from the remainder, it has been repeatedly to the museum that writers and painters, sculptors and poets have returned. In the 21st century, the rich stimuli of museum architecture and Victorian science have continued to engage with modern enquiry, the American artist Mark Dion notably taking Kelvin's pedagogically flowing pitch as a starting point for a productive strand in his output and the achievement, almost exactly half a century ago, of Ian Donald's ultrasound scanner offering a perfect coda to Hunter's investigations into obstetric visualisation two centuries earlier.

Museums are not only about display. Most of The Hunterian's 1.5 million objects are now stored in a remarkable new research and teaching facility at Kelvin Hall. Hunterian Friends and our many other supporters continue to support the development of our collections and the many ways they are encountered in our public galleries and our teaching laboratories. At Kelvin Hall, scientists, artists, writers, and poets, can enjoy the unique rewards of sharing close proximity with astonishing objects, eliciting new avenues of imaginative enquiry and prompting uniquely creative ways of thinking and communicating.

Mungo Campbell
Deputy Director, The Hunterian

The Hunterian Museum Poems

In his essay, 'Modigliani's Alphabet of Love', John Berger tells us something perennially pertinent to what we do in an art gallery and suggests the similarity and difference between that and what we do in a museum: 'Only by considering a painting's method, the practice of its transformation, can we be confident about the direction of its image, the direction of its image's passage towards us and past us. Every painting comes from far away (many fail to reach us) yet we only receive a painting fully if we are looking in the direction from which it has come. This is why seeing a painting is so different from seeing an object.'

Berger's point is to distinguish between the painting and the object and how we might see and understand each, yet is the distinction as clear as that? Certainly, 'seeing a painting' and receiving it fully involves considering its method and where it comes from, and that means paying attention to the artist's creative practice. Seeing an object created by nature, or an engineer or a scientist, rather than an artist, might involve different kinds of appreciation, but it's surely equally necessary to think about where it has come from, to imagine its direction of travel, to receive it most fully where we are now.

In 2015, I edited a book entitled *The Hunterian Poems: An Anthology of Poems to Paintings from the collection of The Hunterian at the University of Glasgow*. I invited a range of poets to write in response to one or more of the paintings in the Hunterian Art Gallery. I had three priorities in mind: there should be as many women as men, there should be representation of the three languages in which most of our literature has been composed, Gaelic, Scots and English, and there should be a diversity of poetic forms, voices, structures, styles, perspectives. In the event, these directives – I can't call them criteria – were more or less comprehensively met and the little book that came from the gathering, beautifully designed and published by Freight Books, was received with some approval. It was suggested that a sequel might be a good idea, a follow-through book which took a similar procedure but addressed the collection in the Hunterian Museum. This would be a very different enterprise, and the result is the book you are holding now.

Looking at a painting normally requires you to stand still or sit facing it, to pay attention to its surface in all its textural complexity, subtleties and boldness of colour and form, its allusions to what it depicts and its hinterland of cultural history and reference. Looking at an object, a sculpture, a work of engineering, a natural structure like a bird's nest or a piece of coral, a fossil or a chunk of stone, is different. To experience and study the works in the Hunterian Museum is to engage in a different way from the way we look at paintings. Normally you'd want to look at an object from more than one position, walk around it, see how its contours connect and separate, study how its form works in three-dimensional space.

Pause on those three dimensions: left-and-right, up-and-down, back-and-forth – and the fourth dimension, time, is also present when you look at an object, in a different way from its presence when you look at a painting. When you look at a painting, time is stilled for the length of your study. When you look at an object, time is part of your moving around it, so on every occasion when you do so, you can begin in a slightly different place and move around it in different directions. This gives your understanding of objects a stake in your understanding of history. The first object in response to which our first poem was written, the fossil of the Bearsden Shark from c.330,000,000 BC, is a particularly daunting example of this.

Once again, John Berger, in another essay, 'Steps Towards a Small Theory of the Visible' (1995), describes the work of painting like this: 'Painting is, first, an affirmation of the visible which surrounds us and which continually appears and disappears. Without the disappearing, there would be perhaps no impulse to paint, for then the visible itself would possess the surety (the permanence) which painting strives to find. More directly than any other art, painting is an affirmation of the existent, of the physical world into which mankind has been thrown.'

That 'affirmation of the existent' takes place in an instant, even if there are decades of experience and practice behind the artist's work and the viewer's understanding of it. The moment of that affirmation happens within time, marking a significance. It is a punctuation point in the multivalent narratives history is made of. By contrast, when you walk around an object, while you're engaging with history by constructing meanings through your own movement, you're also aware, even if hardly conscious of, the history of space. Spatial dimensions operate on objects and our viewing of them differently from spatial relations between a viewer and a painting.

So what we're dealing with is a complementarity. These are the final frontiers of experience. Time (not space) really is the final frontier, for it's always closing in. Time is where you stay and wait. Space is what you move into and explore. Space always means expansion. Time always means negotiation, compromise. Both might need speed, quickness, immediacy; both might need patience, endurance, responsible discretion. But their differences are clearly seen in the responses of engagement each demands, which brings us to The Hunterian Collection.

The invitation was made to poets to respond to a chosen artefact, some thing, an object, either a structure designed in the natural world, or something humanly designed, whether as a sculpture in the broadest sense (like a sarcophagus) or a work of mechanical engineering or an artefact that has both aesthetic and utilitarian purpose, like Verbiest's *Map of the Whole World*. There are any number of objects to choose from, and many of those on permanent display are on The Hunterian pages of the University of Glasgow website. They include the mummy sarcophagus of Lady Shep-en-hor, some deep sea coral, altars and gravestones from forts on the Antonine Wall, artefacts from excavations at brochs and other settlements of the Scottish Iron Age, material evidence of the development of human activity in Scotland and Western Europe from the earliest hunters and fishermen to medieval times. Coins and medals, items of anatomy, rocks and minerals, dinosaurs and fossils, scientific and medical instruments, archaeology, zoology, world cultures, the possibilities are not endless, but it's difficult to think of some aspect of world history that isn't represented in some way by something in the Museum.

The poets responded with eager but cautious appetite. This was to be a very different project from the ekphrastic exercise, poems to paintings. There seemed to be less precedent and fewer examples to follow. All the better, I thought: let's see what happens. In the event, the yield was richer and more varied than I could have predicted, and while each poet responded in her or his idiosyncratic individuality, the assembled works amount to a comprehensive guide – or, rather than guide, introduction to and exploration of the collection in ways that ask questions and open enquiries rather than offer conclusions. These poems are investigations into the provenances of what's held in the Museum.

The anthology is in seven sections with a prelude to take us through the doors and into the collection itself. We begin with some of the world's 'Oldest Things', fossils and footprints from living things far distant in time, but then open our consideration to 'Natural History'. The prospect here marks an affinity of structure, nature's designs, in coral, nests, or animal bone structures, far more intricate and subtle, vulnerable and strong, than anything humans have ever devised. We travel then from Scotland around the world to India, Egypt and China, taking in the simplest and most necessary functional – and decorative – things, an arrowhead, crannogs, the beads found in what remains of crannogs, commemorative sculptures, material reminders of the immaterial, spiritual world, and a map of the whole world, a beautiful but inevitably failed attempt at a totalising comprehension. Then we come into the world of the Romans in Scotland: an imperial authority remembered in artefacts that tell us now of the people who made them and the people and principles to which they refer, sometimes most memorable because of their defiance of imperial rule. Part Five marks the move of the collection, from Glasgow's East End to Gilmorehill, visualised in a painting by Jemima Blackburn. And with that relocation, we enter modernity, the world in which science begins to take precedence: engineering, medicine, artifice of different kinds, yet every example connected to what might be of benefit, long-term, to humans. At its best this is a world not of exploitation but of enlightenment, enquiry that might benefit not only mankind but the whole ecology of an earth we are still only coming to know. Finally, a retrospective look over the whole collection is marked by a portrait of William Hunter himself.

This anthology is at the opposite end of the spectrum from an accountant's evaluation of the collection's itemised worth. It's a compendium of unanswered questions, speculations and promptings, provisional sketches, walkings-around, contemplations, considerations of objects that travel through time as they take you on a walk around the museum, literally if you'd like to, a guide-book for the curious, folk who like to ask about things, people who possess what the first poet in our collection, Edwin Morgan, had in spades: 'the intrinsic optimism of curiosity' – because all museums contain, and are, cabinets of curiosity.

One might say, in fact, that only optimists enter museums. They're places for discoverers and pioneers. Collecting may be a pathology in itself – as John Fowles would describe in his novel, *The Collector* – but there's more than one reason to collect things and a cabinet of curiosities has more than one possible use. The worst of 'collection' is acquisition and the solitary, unshared amplitude of the collector's prized wealth. The best is connectivity: structures of nature connect with structures of the mind, structures of imagination, and structures of science. In the understanding of such connectivity, the priority of numbering may be levelled to relative redundancy. It does not pertain in any primary sense. It is vital and valuable, required and of palpable use, but it is not the only thing, and its use requires its own complementarity: the creative imagination.

And this is what you'll find at work in this book – not simply the creative imagination, but the creative imagination at work in this context, with these things. One of the frequently-quoted proverbial maxims for which Lord Kelvin is famous, is this: 'I often say that when you can measure what you are speaking about, and express it in numbers, you know something about it; but when you cannot measure it, when you cannot express it in numbers, your knowledge is of a meagre and unsatisfactory kind. If you cannot measure it, you cannot improve it.'

He was wrong, of course. (Just as wrong as when he said X-rays would prove a hoax and machines heavier than air could never fly). Numbers only help in certain ways. But they are the normal recourse of those who would seek to catalogue, categorise and exploit. At some level and in some unknowable way, artists and poets are intrinsically opposed to this, perhaps not explicitly, but intrinsically, in our practice. In the Prologue to *Thus Spoke Zarathustra*, Friedrich Nietzsche said it like this: 'one must still have chaos within oneself, to give birth to a dancing star.'

This book proposes that it is the least productive method to seek to impose absolute order on chaos but the most creative practice is to bring the potential of unpredicted imaginations into the order of creation's curation and explore, to learn from what order there is, and see what sparks may fly.

Alan Riach
Professor of Scottish Literature, University of Glasgow

Acknowledgements

The editor would like to thank especially Lee Scott, Harriet Gaston and John Faithfull of The Hunterian and Rob Fairley for permission to include Jemima Blackburn's painting, *Moving the Contents of the Old College Museum* which is reproduced in his book, *Jemima: the Paintings and Memoirs of a Victorian Lady* (Edinburgh: Canongate, 1988).

The Hunterian Museum Poems was made possible through the support of The Hunterian Friends, the Andrew Tannahill Fund for Scottish Literature at the University of Glasgow, GU Heritage Retail Ltd, and through the good will, expertise and enthusiasm of Professor David Gaimster, former Director of The Hunterian, Mungo Campbell, Deputy Director of The Hunterian and Deborah Bennett, Chair of The Hunterian Friends.

Hunterian Friends enjoy unlimited free access to Hunterian Museum and Art Gallery special exhibitions and a varied programme of exclusive events led by The Hunterian Director and curatorial colleagues while supporting the nation's leading university museum and one of Scotland's most important cultural assets. The entire collection cared for by The Hunterian was the first to be recognised as a Collection of National Significance to Scotland. Built on William Hunter's founding bequest, the collections include scientific instruments used by James Watt, Joseph Lister and Lord Kelvin; outstanding Roman artefacts from the Antonine Wall; major natural sciences holdings; one of the world's greatest numismatic collections; impressive ethnographic objects from the Pacific Ocean; a major collection of Scottish art; and one of the UK's top six graphic art collections. The Hunterian is also home to the world's largest permanent display of the work of James McNeill Whistler, the largest single holding of the work of Charles Rennie

Mackintosh and The Mackintosh House, the reassembled interiors from his Glasgow home. Hunterian Friends give vital support and make a direct contribution towards new exhibitions and galleries, education and conservation work, and to new acquisitions.

The Andrew Tannahill Fund for the Furtherance of Scottish Literature was established at the University of Glasgow in 2006 and has supported contemporary writing and cultural debate, historical scholarship into work from the 21st back to the 14th centuries and further. The Tannahill Fund was established by Dr Mabel Tannahill, herself a graduate of the University of Glasgow, in memory of her father Andrew Tannahill, and was launched with a handsome publication of his selected poems, songs and translations, *A Tapsalteerie Touer* (Kettillonia). This may be purchased from Kettillonia publications (www.kettillonia.co.uk). Building on this, the Fund will support further lectures on the interconnectedness of Scottish literature and the other arts, individual research students' bursaries at the University of Glasgow, subsidies towards creative writing colloquia, scholarly research and publications and literary festivals. It is hoped that as the Fund grows it will be able to extend its support across a range of activities related to Scottish literature and language, and to this end donations from all interested parties would be gratefully received and acknowledged. For further information, please contact the University of Glasgow Development and Alumni Office.

We are grateful to Hamish Whyte, Mariscat Press and the Edwin Morgan Estate for permission to reproduce *The Bearsden Shark*.

The Poets

Sheena Blackhall (b.1947) was educated in Aberdeen, took a degree in Psychology with the Open University (1995) and gained an M.Litt with distinction from Aberdeen University (2000). She has been Creative Writing Fellow in Scots at Aberdeen University, 1998-2003, and Creative Writing Tutor at the Institute for Irish and Scottish Studies there in 2007. She is author of novellas, Scots books for bairns, short story collections and many books and pamphlets of poems.

Gerry Cambridge is an essayist, print and publication designer, blues-harmonica player and editor and publisher of *The Dark Horse*, a transatlantic poetry magazine, focusing mainly of Scottish and American poetry. He has published seven poetry collections and worked extensively in schools. The long poem published as a pamphlet, *blue sky, green grass,* won the Callum Macdonald Memorial Award in 2004.

Jim Carruth (b.1963) has had six well-received pamphlet collections of poetry since his first, *Bovine Pastoral* in 2004. He has won both the James McCash poetry competition and the McLellan poetry prize and was awarded a Robert Louis Stevenson Fellowship in 2009. His words have been etched in stone as part of Andy Scott's *Kelpies* sculpture. He was appointed Glasgow Poet Laureate in July 2014 and his first full collection *Killochries* was published in 2015. He is current chair of *St Mungo's Mirrorball* (the Glasgow poetry network) and artistic adviser for the StAnza poetry festival.

Christine De Luca lives in Edinburgh. She writes in English and in Shetlandic, her mother tongue. She was appointed Edinburgh's Makar for 2014-2017. Besides several children's stories and one novel, she has had six poetry collections and four bi-lingual volumes published (French, Italian, Icelandic and Norwegian). She's participated in many festivals in Scotland and abroad and has travelled to Russia, Italy, Iceland as well as Colonsay and Shetland. She has been one of Edinburgh's Shore Poets since 1993.

Lesley Duncan As poetry editor of *The Herald* newspaper, Lesley Duncan has for more than two decades chosen and introduced the newspaper's popular daily poem feature. Her own collection, *Images Not Icons,* was published in 2010, as were two poetry pamphlets on Scottish historical themes. Her own poetry has been published in her newspaper, online, and in a number of anthologies. She has co-edited various anthologies, including the major *Edinburgh Book of Twentieth-Century Scottish Poetry* (with the late Maurice Lindsay), *The Wallace Muse* (with Elspeth King) and (with Alan Riach) *The Smeddum Test*, a compilation of 21st-century poetry in Scots from the annual McCash Poetry Competition. In 2014 she was made an Honorary Fellow of the Association for Scottish Literary Studies. She is currently working on two new books, one about her journalistic career, the other a poetry collection called *Vocalise.*

Gerrie Fellows has published five collections of poetry, most recently *The Body in Space* (Shearsman). Several of her books are sequences investigating how we are changed by our relationship to the technologies around us, from the concrete processes of 20th-century engineering to the more intimate technologies of fertility treatment. A New Zealander by birth, she ran writing workshops for the University of Glasgow for many years and has mentored a number of Glasgow's new poets as part of the Clydebuilt mentoring scheme.

Bashabi Fraser is a poet and children's writer. She has several publications and has been widely anthologised. Her recent publications include *Thali Katori: An Anthology of Scottish & South Asian Poetry*, co-edited with Alan Riach (2017), *The Homing Bird*

(2017) and *Letters to My Mother and Other Mothers* (2015). Her awards include the Saltire Society Outstanding Woman of Scotland (2015). She is Professor of English and Creative Writing and Director of the Scottish Centre of Tagore Studies (ScoTs) at Edinburgh Napier University. She lives and writes in Edinburgh.

Jane Goldman is a Reader in English Literature at the University of Glasgow and a General Editor of the Cambridge University Press edition of the works of Virginia Woolf. Her most recent book on Woolf is *With You in the Hebrides: Virginia Woolf and Scotland* (2013). Her poems have appeared in *Gutter, Scree, Blackbox Manifold, Tender* and other magazines, and her first slim volume is *Border Thoughts* (2014), 'a little theatrical box of spectacle and light [...] the living underworld of Brecht's *Threepenny Opera* translated into raucous girlish post-war wayward ways' – Lisa Jeschke, *Hix Eros*.

John Glenday (b.1952). John Glenday's most recent collection *The Golden Mean* (Picador 2015) won the Roehampton Poetry Prize and was shortlisted for the Saltire Scottish Poetry Book of the Year, 2016. His previous collection *Grain* (Picador, 2009) was a Poetry Book Society Recommendation and shortlisted for both the Ted Hughes Award and the Griffin International Poetry Prize.

Jen Hadfield was born in Cheshire and home is Shetland, whose landscape and natural life persistently informs her work. Her second poetry book Nigh-No-Place (2008, Bloodaxe Books) won the T.S.Eliot Prize in 2008. Her third poetry collection, Byssus, was published by Picador in early 2014. In 2016-17, she was the Writer-in-Residence for the University of Glasgow and the Glasgow School of Art, supported by Creative Scotland. Twitter: @hadfield_jen

Diana Hendry is a poet, short story writer and author of many children's books. She worked as a journalist and English teacher, as a tutor in creative writing for the University of Bristol, the Open

University and the Arvon Foundation, and has won a number of awards, including first prize in the 1996 Housman Society Competition. She was awarded a Robert Louis Stevenson fellowship in 2007 and has been a co-editor of the annual anthology *New Writing Scotland* (2015-17). Her most recent publications are *The Seed-Box Lantern: New & Selected Poems* (Mariscat, 2013) and *My Father as an Ant & Other Stories* (Postbox Press, 2017).

David Kinloch (b.1959) is from Glasgow and is currently Professor of Poetry and Creative Writing at the University of Strathclyde, Glasgow. He is the author of six collections of poetry, most recently *In Search of Dustie-Fute* (Carcanet, 2017), and of many studies in the fields of French, Translation and Scottish Studies.

Pàdraig MacAoidh / Peter Mackay is a native Gaelic speaker from the Isle of Lewis and lectures in the School of English at the University of St Andrews. He has an MA from the University of Glasgow and a PhD from Trinity College, Dublin. He is the author of a book on Sorley MacLean (2010), has co-edited a collection of essays on modern Scottish and Irish poetry and, with Ian S. MacPherson, co-edited *An Leabhar Liath / The Light Blue Book,* an anthology of Scottish Gaelic love and 'transgressive' poetry (2016). His first collection, *Gu Leòr / Galore* was published in 2015.

Aonghas MacNeacail (b. 1942), poet, journalist, broadcaster, scriptwriter, librettist, song-writer and translator, writing in his native Gaelic, and in English. His poetry collections have been published in both languages, and poems anthologised all over the world, translated into many languages, including German, Italian, Irish Gaelic, French, Hebrew, Finnish and Serbo-Croat. He has read his work in Russia, Japan, Poland, Israel, Trinidad, the U.S.A., Canada, and throughout Western Europe. He won the Scottish Writer of the Year Stakis Prize with his third collection, *Oideachadh Ceart / A Proper Schooling and other poems* (Polygon). He has collaborated with many of Scotland's finest composers, including Phil Cunningham, Donald Shaw, William Sweeney and Ronald Stevenson.

Richie McCaffery (b.1986) completed his PhD at the University of Glasgow on the Scottish Poets of World War Two and his essays have appeared in *The Scottish Literary Review, The Dark Horse, Northwords Now* and *Fras*. His poems have been published in journals, e-zines and anthologies, including Salt's *Best British Poetry 2012*, and his pamphlet collections *Spinning Plates* (2012) and *Ballast Flint* (2013) were followed by his first collection *Cairn* (2014).

Peter McCarey (b.1956) Born and raised in Scotland, Peter McCarey ran the language service of the World Health Organisation in Geneva for fifteen years and is now up to various ploys. Founding member of www.makaronic.ch (Geneva), which has just completed its seventh annual show of poetry, music, sound, dance and video performances and installations. Check out www.thesyllabary.com; *Collected Contraptions* (Carcanet, 2012); and *Find an Angel and Pick a Fight* (Molecular Press, 2013), which was commended by the *London Review of Books* as 'intermittently barmy'.

James McGonigal (b. 1947) studied English at the University of Glasgow in the late 1960s. He became a school teacher, teacher educator and latterly Professor of English in Education, publishing in both disciplines. His poetry collections include the prize-winning *Passage / An Pasaiste* (2004) and *Cloud Pibroch* (2010), *The Camphill Wren* (2016) and *Turning Over in a Strange Bed* (2017). A friend and literary executor of Edwin Morgan, he wrote *Beyond the Last Dragon: A Life of Edwin Morgan* (2012) and co-edited *The Midnight Letterbox* (2016), a selection of the poet's correspondence 1950–2010.

Edwin Morgan (1920-2010) One of the major poets of the 20th century. Poet Laureate of Glasgow (1999-2004) and first-ever appointed Scots Makar (National Poet of Scotland), 2004-2010.

Collected Poems (Carcanet, 1996); *Collected Translations* (Carcanet, 1996); *A.D. A Trilogy of Plays on the Life of Jesus Christ* (Carcanet, 2000); *Cathures* (Carcanet, 2002); *The Play of Gilgamesh* (Carcanet, 2005); *Beyond the Sun: Scotland's Favourite Paintings* (Luath, 2007); *Dreams and Other Nightmares* (Mariscat, 2010).

Liz Niven (b.1952) is a Glasgow-born, Dumfries-based poet, writing in English and Scots. Collections include *Stravaigin, Burning Whins* and *The Shard Box* (Luath Press). *Scots Language in Education* (Mercator: Netherlands). Awards include the McCash Poetry Prize, Year of the Artist and Times Ed / Saltire for ground-breaking work in Scots Language in Education. She has collaborated with artists, sculptors and photographers in text-based installations. Honorary Fellow of the Association for Scottish Literary Studies.

Donny O'Rourke is a poet, songwriter, film maker, critic, editor, teacher and translator, born, brought up and educated in Renfrewshire, with degrees from the Universities of Glasgow and Cambridge. After several years working in television, he edited the landmark anthology *Dream State: The New Scottish Poets* (1994, revised and updated 2001). His own collections include *The Waistband* (1997) and *On a Roll: A Jena Notebook* (2001).

Janet Paisley is a poet, novelist, playwright and scriptwriter, writing in Scots and English. Her work has been translated into German, Russian, Lithuanian, Slovak, Catalan, Spanish, Hungarian, Ukranian, Italian, Portuguese and Dutch and is widely anthologised. Her critically-acclaimed historical novels, *White Rose Rebel* and *Warrior Daughter*, are published as Penguin paperbacks. Her new collection is *Sang fur the Wandert* from Luath Press.

Richard Price (b.1966) is a poet who moves easefully between the lyrical and the avant-garde. His collections include *Lucky Day* (2004) and *Greenfields* (2007), and he has edited the intermittent poetry pamphlet *printed / spoken*. He is the author of the novel *The Island* (2010) and a short story collection, *A Boy in Summer* (2002). From 2003 to 2010 he was Head of Modern British Collections and is now Head of Content and Research Strategy at the British Library, London.

John Purser (b.1942) has published four books of poetry, the most recent being *There Is No Night: New and Selected Poems* (Kennedy & Boyd, 2014). His poetry has also appeared in many magazines and anthologies. Of his six radio plays commissioned by the BBC, *Carver* won a Giles Cooper Award and was published by Methuen. In 1992 his book *Scotland's Music* won him the McVitie Scottish Writer of the Year Prize. Purser is a Researcher at Sabhal Mòr Ostaig, the Gaelic College on Skye.

Alan Riach (b.1957) Born in Lanarkshire, Professor of Scottish Literature, University of Glasgow. Books include poetry: *The Winter Book* (2017), *Homecoming* (2009) and *Wild Blue: Selected Poems* (2014); criticism: *Hugh MacDiarmid's Epic Poetry* (1991), *Representing Scotland* (2005), and co-authored with Alexander Moffat, *Arts of Resistance: Poets, Portraits and Landscapes of Modern Scotland* (2008), described in the *Times Literary Supplement* as 'a landmark book', and *Arts of Independence: The Cultural Argument and Why It Matters Most* (2014). Riach and Moffat are also the co-editors of the annotated edition of J. D. Fergusson's radical manifesto-book *Modern Scottish Painting* (1943; new edition, 2015). He is the author, with Moffat and John Purser, of the collection of essays, *Arts and the Nation* (2017).

Alan Spence (b.1947), Glasgow-born poet, playwright, novelist and short story writer, has been practising meditation for more than 40 years. With his wife Janani he runs the Sri Chinmoy Meditation Centre in Edinburgh. His books of fiction include *Its Colours They Are Fine*, *Stone Garden*, *The Magic Flute*, *Way to Go*, *The Pure Land* and *Night Boat*. Poetry collections include *Glasgow Zen*, *Seasons of the Heart*, *Clear Light* and *Morning Glory*. He is Professor Emeritus in

Creative Writing at Aberdeen University, and in 2017 was appointed as Edinburgh Makar.

Gerda Stevenson (b.1956), actor, writer, director, singer-songwriter; poetry, drama and prose widely published, staged and broadcast throughout Britain and abroad; has read her work at international festivals, including Czech Republic, Slovakia, Poland, Trinidad, and Italy; recipient of Scottish Arts Council and Creative Scotland bursaries; her play *Federer versus Murray* (pub. Salmagundi, USA), toured to New York, 2012; nominated Scots Singer of the Year, 2014, for an album of her own songs *Night Touches Day*; her poetry collection *If This Were Real* (Smokestack Books, 2013) published in Italian by Edizioni Ensemble, Rome, 2017. Her second poetry collection, *Quines*, will be published by Luath Press, 2018. www.gerdastevenson.co.uk

Sheila Templeton writes in both Scots and English. She has won the McCash Scots Language Poetry Competition three times and also the Robert McLellan poetry competition. From 2007 to 2010 she was Poet in Residence at the Harbour Arts Centre, Irvine and also had the honour of being Makar of the Federation of Writers Scotland 2009 to 2010. Her collections include *Slow Road Home* (Makar Press, 2004), *Digging for Light* (New Voices Press, 2011), *Tender is the North* (Red Squirrel Press, 2013) and *Gaitherin* (Red Squirrel Press 2016). She has also recently been part of a collaborative translation project which resulted in *Owersettin* (Tapsalteerie Press, 2016) a poetry pamphlet in Scots, Gaelic and English.

Hamish Whyte (b.1947) was a professional librarian at the Mitchell Library in Glasgow and has edited anthologies including *Mungo's Tongues: Glasgow Poems 1630-1990*, *An Arran Anthology* and *Kin: Scottish Poems about Family*. He is the publisher of Mariscat Press, which won the Michael Marks Pamphlet Publisher of the Year Award and the Callum Macdonald Memorial Award in 2015, and for many years published work by Edwin Morgan. His published poems include *Window on the Garden* (2006), *A Bird in the Hand* (2008) and *The Unswung Axe* (2012). His latest publication is *Things We Never Knew* (2016).

The Blackstone Chair, formerly used at the University of Glasgow for examinations, 18th century

Opening the Doors
Alan Riach

First there's the Blackstone Chair, with the hourglass over your head:
Time's limited, and running out, and this is your induction, test:
What can you say within these strict parameters? This will be
What we judge you on. Begin. Let's go –
To bedrock, first: minerals – gifts from the underworld, deep in the
    earth
Blue crystals of caledonite with pyromorphite, greeny-ochre,
And the beautiful turquoise blue, the deeper blue of linarite,
And named for their place of discovery, my birthplace, Lanarkshire,
The lanarkite's transparent shining needles bristle up at you like
    blades:
Rare minerals, recovered, showing how to read the rocks,
The meaning of what's deep inside the mountains:
Metals, gems, tools, pigments, stones with which to build,
From here to the farthest distance, oldest things –
Distance on the earth: from Knoydart, Strontian, Skye,
Arizona, Bombay, Pakistan, Brazil,
Australia, Bolivia, Tennessee, Namibia,
Kilpatrick, Kilsyth, Dumbarton, Ayrshire, Ben Hope –
Colours blue and silver, yellow, green,
Bright from inside, radiating out –
Then rocks from outer space, that come back in,
The farthest-flung, approaching earth, meteorites, arrivals,
Telling us what formed the sun, the planets, all
The vast inhuman cosmos that surrounds us,
Coming in where the chordates rise
(Animals whose flexible support, a rod along the length of them,
Becomes the backbone in vertebrates, the notochord):
Earliest chordates 500 million years ago

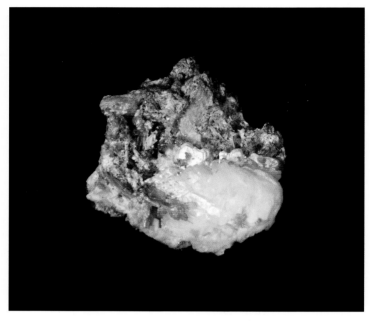

Specimen of leadhillite and caledonite, named after Leadhills and Scotland

(Vertebrates beginning to evolve then, fins to limbs,
Scales to feathers, earliest ancestors still to humans,
Backboned, vertebrate, to 'learn the trick of walking upright here' –
Captain Cook sails into the South Pacific
And that old shark was swimming in the waters
Millions of years before he sailed upon them –
And interstellar space is dark because it's cold out there –
There is no Gaelic word for nation.
Maybe the closest is 'dùthchas': a threefold thing, connecting
And changing through time: Land, people, culture.
Land, as in the whole terrain – seas and archipelagos too –
Scotland for sure but all the whole wide world beside –
Measure it all in the scale of geology, 'deep time' as Hutton said –
People as in, 'eyes in all heads / to be looked out of' –
All through that world and all through time –
And the unthinkable regions beyond –
Culture as in then what's made,
By the land and sea, by the people too, for better and so often too,
For worse. So that which might seem most repellent,
Syphilitic skulls, the murderous parts of the body, turned against
        you,
The unfinished, unformed, the inimical –
All are yet in service, brought in, in a certain way, to help:
Beneficent discovery, ideals of healing, health, the courage to look at
        the worst,
To address the necessary, difficult matters, the questions. –
And so to coins: James Bruce from Larbert, Stirling,
'Abyssinian Bruce' exploring Ethiopia,
Eighteenth-century man, crossing deserts and mountains,
To the source of the Blue Nile,
A journey of more than three years,
And finding in Egypt the Ptolemies gold coins,
To bring them back from the third and second centuries, BC,
To deliver them to William Hunter, for residence, for the Collection:

Roman nails from the Antonine Wall

Gold circles: heads embossed upon each one,
On some, two heads in profile, women, men,
A bird, a cornucopia or horn of plenty,
Brimming with grapes, riches of food and wine, they signify:
Matters of value not to be denied. The coins remain
Quite unremarked by poets, healthy in their mild regard
Or disregard for accountancy – yet they are signals too
Of when such symbols of exchange were vital,
More vital, less overwhelming than the profiteers would have them
            now,
Wherever greed and acquisition reign. Track the signs of money
            through Victoria's reign
To Glasgow's currency, as it was, and history comes to
Always current questions. And so to nails, the Roman nails
That keep their value, practical, historic shapes, designs you'd plan
            to build with,
Make such things secure as have to be, a cabinet, a building, finally
            settle the coffin lid,
When it comes to that. Accumulated signs and signals, read them as
            you will,
Not passively at all. But with some value of disinterestedness,
Analysis, and sympathy. Be curious. Be optimistic. Come to the doors
And look past the Chair to where the contents beckon.
Beckon you in. Come in.

One:
Oldest
Things

The Bearsden Shark, *Akmonistion zangerli,* found in Bearsden in the 1980s by Stan Wood

The Bearsden Shark

Edwin Morgan

O what a whack of a black of a sleek sweet cheeky tail in its big blue
        den
Of water! There were no bears then!
Waterworld it was, warm and salty, wet and scary,
Wild shapes, no ships, no sheep, no sheep-dip, a deep deep, very!
Fish but no fishermen, no fishmen, no kingfishers, no kings,
Fish fishing for fish, yes, anglers, rays, jaws, shocks, wings,
And all those early murky milky things,
Stings on strings, things that spring.
Through shoal and shining flock and froth and freath and freaky
        frisky flashers, like a liner,
The Bearsden shark coasts casually, kinglily, killingly casual, casing
        the scales, lazily pacing and chasing, lord of the place, of
        the plaice, lordly diner.
Little does he know of land and ocean, change and chance,
Little would he care if he knew. Little would he change if he cared.
        Little would he love if he changed it. His is reality without
        remorse or romance.
Heroic long-dead creature, waiting in death
To be discovered, uncovered, recovered, recalled from the cold solid
        soil that never felt your breath:
We have you in a fosse, a fossil, a fragile long-forgotten force of our
        growing, growling, grounded, founded but bounding,
        bonding and unbonding earth.

Trilobite, *Odontochile spinifera*, from Morocco, 395 million years old

Faking It

Jim Carruth

'Faking trilobites is not a new invention'
                    How to identify fake trilobites
                    Jens Koppka, Heiko Sonntag and Horst Burkard

How do I know who you are or claim to be
when pretence can reap such great rewards?

Am I right to be suspicious seeing there in front of me
not the dull black lustre I find in many of your kind

but a variety of reds and browns, unnaturally shiny,
devoid of the cracks, terrace lines on free cheeks

that would mark the stresses of your journey to date;
tubercles, nodes, ridges and pits all smoothed over.

I can see it in your eyes, those individual lenses.
Your little bubbles on the surface are part of the act.

Even this hard bed you lie in doesn't ring true to me.
I'm told using a UV-light might expose what is hidden

or taking a solvent to your short body reveal more.
Some touching up does not cross the line into fraud.

I could bite into you right here and now to test you-
a fake will always feel softer on the teeth than truth.

If all else fails a slice in half with a diamond blade
will once and for all reveal the void beneath the show.

Fine greenockite crystals from the Bishopton railway cutting

Greenockite

Jim Carruth

Named not for the damp coastal town
but for the Lord of the land you were found on.

I nearly missed you today, so small,
swallowed within a dull basalt host:

a cadmium ochre formed millions of years ago
as ground waters washed and cooled the lava flows;

minute honeyed yellow hexagonals
sought after across the world – a rare mineral.

Though such brightness can come at a cost
it lit up the canvasses of Van Gogh

as you do today shining like little beacons at sea
the surrounding rock – a grey overcast sky.

Balanerpeton Woodi
aka Lizzie the Lizard, Bathgate Beast
Sheila Templeton

Yer naethin but a wee tease
you temnospondyl amphibian you –
caain aa they experts heilster gowdie,
luminaries knocked clean aff their pottiestattur
   – thinkin ye were a reptile.
The hale warld o paleontology turned dizzy
tae think reptiles daundered aboot
the steamy equitorial swamps
o Bathgate – millions o years
afore onybody thocht they existed.
Romer's Gap wud niver be the same.
Aa the evidence wis there:
yer dainty set o straight ribs
buccal respiration gulping air
straight intae yer mou
yer land lovin legs – even ears
that could hear high frequency soond.
But na, na. Ye hud them fooled.
An nae content wi that
 – ye ill-trickit wee amphibian –
tae hide yersel in a dry stane dyke
nae een yer hale sel – but discreet
wee bitties, in twa halves
jist eneuch tae titillate.
It took Stan Wood
fossil hunter byordnar
tae fankle ye oot o that lair.

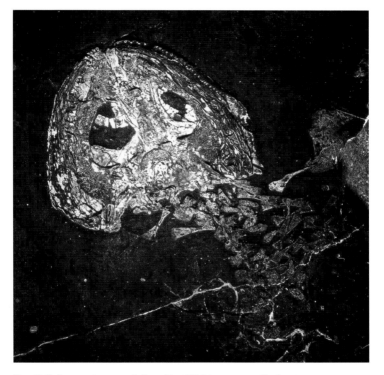

Fossil, *Balanerpeton woodi*, from East Kirkton quarry, Bathgate

An he thocht yer teeth
were contained within the matrix
of the negative half.
Ha! Whit did he ken? Thon wis
naethin but a sleekit smirk on yer phizog.

The world's smallest dinosaur footprint, found on Skye, Middle Jurassic

The World's Smallest Dinosaur Footprint

Gerry Cambridge

Some minute out of time
before shop and love and word
the dainty dinosaur
no bigger than a blackbird
Left this single print
immortalised in stone,
like the foot of a miniature duck:
the enigmatic, lone
Insignia of its passing
one hundred and seventy million years ago —
its great one-word poem
it did not know

It wrote, chasing the end of life,
and did not care
in any case
destined for mud and air

Two:
Natural History

Deep sea coral, *Lophelia pertusa*

Deep Sea Coral, Lophelia Pertusa
Gerda Stevenson

I'm a fish oot o watter noo, strandit
in the lichtit drocht o a gless kist
fur fowk tae gaup at; an amputatit bit,
that driftit frae hame –
the Darwin Mounds, thon ocean airt
whilk lay ayont kennin o mankind
sin the ice age, faddoms deep, till,
no lang syne, a ship cam by,
nearhaund tae Scotia's western shores,
an fund a wunner o the warld:
a cradle o laced banes, ruitit in saund
piled heich as bens, braid as kye faulds,
and aulder nor the pyramids.

I lang fur the glisterin gliff o scales and fins,
flittin atween my brainched limbs;
I wis pairt o a livin skeleton whilk grows
and grows, biggit slaw ower time
aneath the ocean swaws, howdie tae life,
teemin like ferlie pairlins in daurk howes –

gif lat alane, mind, ainerly gif lat alane:
fur aince ye herry and smatter sic treisur
wi yer hankerin eftur gowd,
yon jizzen bed and bield is deid fur aye.

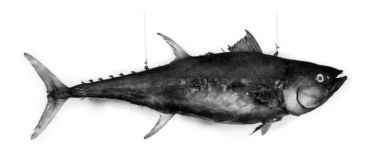

Bluefin tuna, *Thunnus thynnus*, 19th century

Scouler's Tuna
Jim Carruth

Glorious in your prime all power and streamline fin
ten feet from nose to tail, slicing through currents

Your kind praised from the lips of Aristotle and Pliny,
but in terms of survival size isn't everything.

A poor sense of direction paired with greed
brought your downfall: lost in the Clyde estuary,

trapped in the same net as the herring you hunted,
comic giant surrounded by silver Lilliputians.

Centuries later you hang on wires from the ceiling
a gentle sway in the updraft of a faulty air conditioner.

At first wrongly described as fine mackerel, now named
after the man who bought your corpse from the docks.

Your only legacy is captured in the faded sign
Thought to be the oldest stuffed tuna in the world.

Tree snail shells, *Polymita picta*

Philosophical Instruments
Jen Hadfield

At dusk, punctuation falls upon the garden.
Bait the wall and wait. Here in a rockandrolling
wagon-trail come the snails
crushed too tenderly
to die, ready to tumble eyes first
anyway into whatever the future holds: spicy
saws, this fine Yell strawberry,
this grapefruit peel.

Snails, I'm learning from you.

Crest the event horizon with antennae
outstretched, like gum on a boot, then,
like philosopher's compasses, spread further,
exceeded by the fruit, bumping
your question against your scarlet holy mountain
before you fall on it, in
slowly breaking
waves

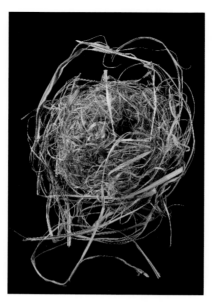

Harvest mouse, *Micromys minutus* and nest

The Machine for Making Epiphanies
David Kinloch

The machine for making epiphanies
is unsuspended
it hangs in space as Earth once did

before the second bang. Provenance
unknown, accession date obscure,
its 'isn't thereness' inflames

museum air; you move to kiss
it as a reliquary, your body
reflected in its silvery skeleton

but glimpse instead the straw
nest of a harvest mouse,
'micromys minutus',

leaves and stibble,
foggage green or ribbons
all stray and wisp about

the dark hole at its heart.

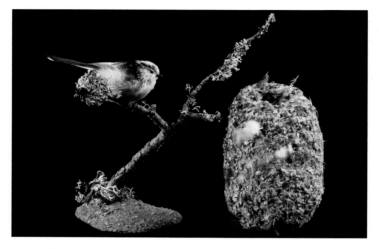

Long-tailed tit taxidermy mount and nest, *Aegithalos caudatus*

Long-tailed Tit and Nest
Gerry Cambridge

Taken away, taken clean away
out of the enormous, intricate
Maytime woods and thickets,
extending for miles around
and constantly in motion,
the breezes rippling the billion leaves,
the bumblebees
blundering here and there
among celandine and ladysmock,
the processional white clouds ...
Here, all by itself on its bare perch,
along with the little masterpiece
of felted moss and spider silk
lined with a thousand feathers
and patched with lichen scraps
in its unchanging ecosystem:
floating hearts, a slice of brain
sawn from a frozen head,
the cabinets of arrested butterflies,
phalanxes of stilled beetles,
the dentist drill bits, knives, and saws...

I step into dank November
where leaves rain down in twirling throngs
and every day I hear its living fellows
flit in their chirring groups
about the wintered woods
clinging to twigs with tiny claws

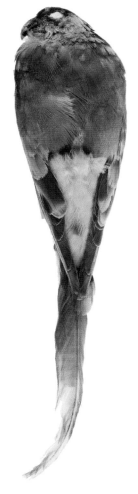

Bird cabinet skin: Paradise parakeet, *Psephotus pulcherrimus*

Feathers and Fur
Jim Carruth

Bird cabinet skin: Paradise parakeet
(Psephotus pulcherrimus)

'No one can see it without desiring to possess so beautiful and
graceful a bird, and large sums are constantly being paid for
handsome specimens by amateurs; but alas! one in a dozen survives
a few months and dies suddenly in a fit.'

Parrots in Captivity – William Thomas Greene

All we are left with is this extraordinary plumage
lifeless feathers of turquoise, aqua and scarlet.

It flew across the river valleys of New South Wales:
forests full of eucalyptus, ironbarks and bloodwoods,

small family groups, feasting on grass seed
ground loving, making their nests in termite mounds,

but suffered cattle and pasture, slash and burn of man
who marvelled at its beauty and longed to cage it.

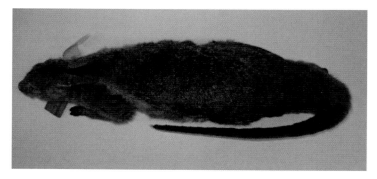

Cabinet skin: Nail-tailed/bridled wallaby, *Onychologea fraenata*

Cabinet Skin: Nail-tailed/bridled wallaby
(Onychologea fraenata)

At times the final bell toll can be premature
so relatives of this bridled nail-tail wallaby,

which has been trapped, exported North
kept in drawers, skin flattened like road kill

moved from museum to dusty museum
wrongly labelled by one as a kangaroo

then classified as extinct for decades,
have re-emerged and remember us.

Three:
Round the World from Scotland: India, Egypt China

Flint arrowheads found at Stoniehall, Firth, Orkney
Image courtesy Dr Hugo Anderson-Whymark

Arrowhead

(*Stoniehall, Firth, Orkney, 151AD*)
Janet Paisley

The stone that rings is the one to strike,
the one that splits to the hammer blow.

From that core, I chip a slice, grip
with leather mitt. Push, and turn,
push. Flakes of flint fall in the bowl
between my thighs. The knapping shards
too small for use, dangerous to feet
and flesh, will be buried in the pit.
Push, and turn. The antler tip gouges
out the sharper edge of arrowhead.

I have made six, this one the last.
When it is done, they will be bound
to feathered shafts, blessed for flight,
for their return, barb bedded deep
in bird or beast, bringers of death,
and food, and life – the hunters praised,
as I am prized for nimble fingers,
a girl who hopes, one day, to hunt.

I weigh the weapon in my hand, wish
for many flights, to strike tomorrow.

Amber bead with inscription 'crannog' on reverse

Crannogs
Richard Price

Writing is taking so long –
by the time I've reached this line-end
the how of all the sensate nodes
in my entire small universe
transmitting, coming back,
to all the sensate nodes
in my entire small universe
                          has dissolved.

                    I've
lost my grasp,
of all those fast drives past
                    an Ayrshire crannog
with a someone, a certain someone

and the same for a single journey to a Uist crannog
with a different certain someone
(years later –

don't ask me
        for archaeological details –)

                    and now I'm folding myself in,
                    curling myself up, trying
                    trying to let my Ayrshire someone go,
                    even now, trying to let this anger go,
                    and folding myself in, compacted,
                    praying my Uist someone will survive,
                    even now, trying to let this love go,

let love forgive itself – and I don't pray –

and now I'm the ruins
of a Renfrewshire crannog,
remains, stumps in the shallows
of a huge river,
letting the moon's force
slowly destroy me
and keep my thoughts
safe

(from the senses
            and confession)

Amber bead with inscription 'crannog' on reverse

Marble figure of Hindu deity Ganesh

Ganesha
Alan Spence

I'm not an animal, I'm not a man,
I am a god - I Am since time began.
God of Beginnings, Guardian at the Gate,
I'm Lord of Thresholds, transcend time and fate.

What you see is the form that I assume.
Here I am, the elephant in the room -
proboscis, tusks, pot belly, flapping ears.
Light on my feet, I'll dance away your fears.

Ganesha, Remover of Obstacles,
performer of everyday miracles.
Your children know me well, each avatar -
I'm Horton, Dumbo, Kala Nag, Babar.

But yes, those obstacles - who put them there?
Now, offer me your mantra, homage, prayer.
Aum Ganeshaya Nama - chant my name.
Aum Ganeshaya Nama - chant my name.

Egyptian clay model of a woman and child, 1000-600 BC

Mother and Child

John Glenday

You find yourself awake, in a bed
that is not your own, in a room you do not recognise,
in a city where you are a stranger

and there beside you, the daughter who has never lived.
While you aged, she continued to grow,
though the dead cannot grow,

they can only grow closer.
Her name, if she ever had one, would be your name.
All those years without sleep.

Remember how she stirred in you once,
heavy as the shifting tide. For as long as you live
she will draw in your breath,

cancel out your warmth,
compound every silence; in that bed,
in that room, in that city you have never visited.

Egyptian mummy, the Lady Shep-en-hor, 600 BC

The Lady Shep-en-hor

Diana Hendry

We can read the journey of her soul to the underworld
on the lid of her sycamore coffin. All being well,
if her heart was proved as light as a feather, and if
she gained passage through the Hall of Judgement
she will have reached the Afterlife long ago.
The coffin's ajar. The guide says we can look inside
at the mummified body left behind. Embarrassed,
we crouch and peep. It feels a bit rude. You have
to believe it's her, bandaged and bundled in
a yellowing sheet. Better to look at all the birds,
eyes, gods and hieroglyphics painted in bright coloured
miniatures on the outside. Such company she keeps!
Here's green-skinned Osiris in his glamorous hat,
Geb, the earth god with his sacred goose, Horus with
the sun in his right eye, the moon in his left and Nut,
goddess of heaven, her welcoming wings spread wide.
A bull is the bearer of Shepenhor's coffin. I think
of Cleopatra's barge drawn down the Cydnus by
attendant mermaids, and then of the lullaby we used
to sing to send drowsy children off to sleep, offering
the moon and stars to play with as long as you don't cry.

Afterwards I go down to the museum's shop, buy
Hieroglyphs from A to Z: a Rhyming Book for Kids.
If you draw a lion, a lasso, a horned viper and a reed
leaf, you've learnt to spell the Egyptian word for love.

Hurrah for Hatshepsut

Lesley Duncan

Sometimes I lie on my bed like a mummy
(Of, naturally, the Egyptian kind
Being maternally already thus defined),
Feeling remote and far from chummy.

This ain't rehearsal for my own sarcophagus;
I'd rather dodge the final boxing fuss,
Believing that a stout black plastic bag
Would do quite nicely for an atheist hag.

No, I see myself as Hatshepsut,
The female pharaoh, kinkily cute,
Sporting her ceremonial beard,
The more to be revered and feared.

I mentally snap my scarab rings
At two-dimensional underlings
And rage in cryptic hieroglyphs
At Nubian slaves with curious quiffs,
Then commune with the great god Ra,
Before reverting to terrestrial ma.

*Note: Hatshepsut was a notable pharaoh of the 18th Dynasty, reigning
from 1503 to 1482 BC. She left an imposing palace across the Nile from
Luxor and was often depicted as a male.*

Lady Shep-en-hor
(Mummie in Hunterian Museum, Glasgow: 600BC)
Liz Niven

Oh, Lady Shep-en-hor,
 wrappt up cosy
in yer brichtlie paintit
coffin cacoon.

Wi Geb, the Earth God,
Horus, God o the Lift;
richt een the sun,
left, the muin.
Offerin protection fae evil
oan intae the efterlife.
Covert in spells an cherms,
multi-colourt as a Shetlan gansey,
tae see ye oan yer wey.

Oh, Lady Shep-en-hor,
waken fae yer lang sleep,
help us oan wir wey noo.
Pairliament or Hoose o Lords an Ladies,
bring alang yer jugs an jewels.
Amphora fillt wi fluid
tae calm wir troublt watters,
jewels tae sperkle licht fae derkness.
Come banish evil een,
muckle mooths wha ding us doon,
harbingers o doom.
Aye, we've muckle tae bury here.
Aleppo tae Alabama,
Calais tae Cork,

Belfast tae Brussels,
Syria tae Soothampton,
Palestine tae Peterheid.

Gie us yer Horus een.
Protect us fae evil.
Gie us spells an cherms,
no fir an efterlife,
jist tae get throu this yin,
Oh, Lady Shep-en-Hor.

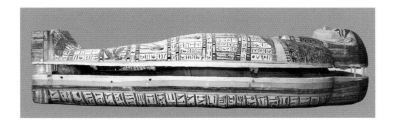

Egyptian mummy, the Lady Shep-en-hor, 600 BC

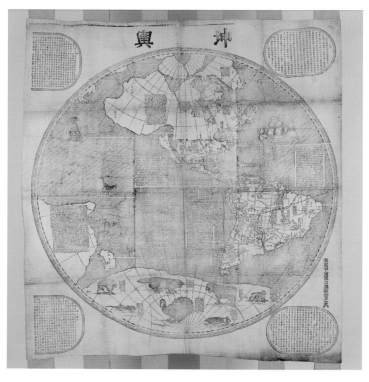

Ferdinand Verbiest, *Kunyu Quantu (A Map of the Whole World)*, 1674

A Map of the Whole World

Christine De Luca

This map was to be impressive: Verbiest's best.
The old Jesuit had studied well, had read of Zheng He,
his voyages, knew of Dutch cartography; of longitude
and latitude; of the Equator and lesser parallels.

He was ready to render oceans, continents, mountains,
plains and rivers; to label coastal features, to add
cartouches with incidental knowledge; to find a place
to fill with animals, a concise bestiary for Kangxi,

his ever-curious Emperor. Perhaps he'd break the
neat billows with galleons, an occasional mermaid.
His hands, cold in the scriptorium, were full of talent.
He had mastered all the characters, the art-form;

was skilled in woodblock, could wield the finest knife
with a rare confidence. He had read many treatises
about inkstones; knew the ingredients that wouldn't fade,
could select the finest paper. And he had much patience.

His map would have two hemispheres; China on the edge,
not centred; and the Americas to the east, beyond Japan
and that rising sun. Finally, the woodblocks would be inked,
the paper pressed across the engraving, then slowly lifted.

He'd hold his breath as his rivers flooded into continents,
mountains rose, coastlines beckoned; as America reached
across to Kamchatka and, in Antarctic menageries, a unicorn
pranced, a turkey flounced and a mighty crocodile shambled.

Hentilagets

Christine De Luca

No dat I'd lippen dee, Verbiest, sae trang wi
da Chinese Emperor, ta ken aboot dis hentilagets
o skerries. Or, for dat maitter, wi der namin.

Even da best map-makkers missed wis oot or,
whan dey fan wis, prammed wis ida Moray Firt
ithin a peerie box. Maistlins we wir jöst owre
da horizon, a vague prospect, *Ultima Thule*.

I canna blame dem, for dat nordern ocean
stipplt apö first maps wis buskit wi wrecks
an sea munsters; hed da likkly o a graveyard.

Hendrik Hondius man a read da starns wi
a Davis quadrant an checkit better charts,
Mercator's, afore he teckled *terra incognito,*
dat *Orcades and Schetlandia* Blaeu engraved.

An sae da box appeared: tree dimensions flatcht
ta twa; latitude an longitude forgien; laand scaled
doon, crubbit up, sae da rest could braethe.

But tap dat box an, boy, we'll loup oot! Gie you
sic a gluff, you'll nivver trust a Verbiest again!
We'll rex wis, i wir ain place, prood an prunk,
boannie as a weel-med gansey, newly dressed.

Hentilagets are tufts of sheep's wool often caught in heather; usually the softest.
Dressing a newly knitted garment involves washing and stretching.

Odds and Ends

Christine De Luca

Not that I'd expect you, Verbiest, so busy with
the Chinese Emperor, to know about these oddments
of skerries. Or, for that matter, with their naming.

Even the best map-makers missed us out or,
when they found us, crammed us into the Moray Firth
in a little box. Mostly we wert just over
the horizon, a vague prospect, *Ultima Thule*.

I cannot blame them, for that northern ocean
stippled on to first maps was decorated with wrecks
and sea monsters; had the appearance of a graveyard.

Hendrik Hondius must have read the stars with
a Davis quadrant and checked better charts,
Mercator's, before he tackled *terra incognito,*
that *Orcades and Schetlandia* Blaeu engraved.

And so the box appeared: three dimensions flattened
into two; latitude and longitude compromised; land scaled
down, confined, so the rest could breathe.

But tap that box and, boy, we'll leap oot! Give you
such a fright, you'll never trust a Verbiest again!
We'll stretch out, in our own place, visible and confident,
beautiful as a well-made jumper, newly finished.

Four:
The Romans in Scotland

Bust of Silenus from Bar Hill Roman Fort, 142-180 AD

Silenus

Donny O'Rourke

The best thing for a man is not to be born, and if already born, to die as soon as possible.

Beef's rare; not as in pink, but short supply.
I pine for suckling pig and pigeon pie.
Tonight it's my turn at the cooking pot.
Turnip, kale and brambles are all we've got.

Bread bulks it out; there's flavour in fish sauce.
With whey- wet cheese, fresh pressed, tough goat's no loss.
Upon whatever foraged fare we dine,
The stomach armies march on wants its wine!

Amphorae and flagons are weapons too.
Who would fraternise with the local brew?
Brother, stupefy this squadron as it sups:
Keep us coarse but comradely in our cups.

Raised middle fingers ward off the evil eye.
Caledonia, like you, is seldom dry.
Bacchus' tutor! Teach rookies how to tope.
Guarding Rome's turf, the grape's their only hope.

Silenus, to you, I propose a toast.
In effigy, watch over this out-post.
Prophesies and stories, inspired by drink?
Libations help lost legions *not* to think.

Each statuette stone- masons had installed,
Showed you old, flat faced, thick lipped, beetle browed: *bald*.
Big bellied, bearded, bless the blind drunks' prayer.
As thanks, new carved: a *Scottish* head of hair.

This sand stone statuette of the minor deity associated with drunkenness was unearthed at Bar Hill Fort near Kilsyth. All representations of Bacchus's mentor found in Scotland, depict the customarily bald Silenus with a thick thatch of hair. The author laments how closely he resembles the wine god's likeness!

cruithneach mi

Aonghas MacNeacail

cruithneach mi

ged is fhada bho'n tùs
a thug beatha dha
mo dhuan 's mo shiubhal

is ged a b' ann tromh'n chloich
a b'fheudar dhut mo choinneachadh
cha dubhar as mo bhith

ged a mhùchadh neart mo theanga
's mo ghràmar a chur fo chidhis bhuan
gus nach cluinnear òran bhuam
's nach robh deasbad air bhilean –
na saoil gu bheil mi dùinte mach a
cuisle dhomhainn d' eachdraidh

oir ged a dh'fhàgar balbh mi,
cunntais mi ameasg do shinnsirean,
tha an gine fhathasd a' gluasad
ann an dorchadas d' fhéithean

ach bha innleachd anns na meòir
a thug mion-ghràbhaladh dha mo chruth
leis an deòn nach b' faileas mi

abrar gur mise fortuna

agus ann an toirt cumadh dha
mo chuimhne, shnaidheadair,
thog thu rath lainnireach dha mo
sgeul, thug thu buannachd dhomh

mo rùine a' biathadh do rùn
gu'm bidhinn 'nam bhànrainn
                      dha'n t-sùil

rath – fortress, good fortune
rùine – mystery

Fountainhead from Bearsden Roman Fort

i am a pict

Aonghas MacNeacail

i am a pict

though it's long since the origin
that gave life to
my ode and my journey

and though it was through stone
you were required to meet me,
my being won't be blacked out

though my tongue's vigour was stifled,
my grammar set under a lasting mask,
till a song could not be heard from me
nor was there debate on lips –
don't think i am excluded from
the deep artery of your history

for though i was left dumb,
you may count me among your ancestors,
the gene is still travelling
in the darkness of your veins

but there was artistry in the fingers
that gave fine carving to my form
with the desire that i be no shadow

it is said that i am fortuna

and in giving shape to
my memory, sculptor,
you built a radiant fortress for my
story, you gave me the reward

my mystery feeding your wish
that i should be a queen
                    to the eye

Terracotta tile with dog footprint from Bothwellhaugh Roman Fort

Remains

Hamish Whyte

We love clues
to the invisible:

from a workman's hands
imprinted in concrete
on the Dundas Street
pavement

to this broken
terracotta tile
found near the Antonine
Wall bearing
the unmistakable mark
of a dog's paw.

The *Antonine Wall* display in the Hunterian Museum

Antonine Wall

Bashabi Fraser

Walking into this silent space
Between towering pillars
That once bolstered miles
Of walls that ran
From the reflective
Forth to the restless Clyde,
One has to stand still to
Listen to the marching feet
Of men from Syria, Spain or Algeria,
The legionary and the auxiliary
The captured and the coerced –
Soldiers of a mighty empire
Pushing the frontier between
The bonnie banks of freedom's streams.

This was a mighty feat
Of seventeen forts and
Many watchtowers to defeat
The Caledonian in their own land
And keep them safely
On the other side of glory.

What would Agricola think
Today to see his architectural
Dream fragmented and dispersed,
Assigned to the historical glamour
Of archaeological splendour?

It can speak across the
North Sea to another Wall
That came down recently
And stands with reverence
In Berlin's museum arcade
For spectators who come to
Revel in what was their
Decision to dismantle and disperse
As walls must, when emperors
Leave, be willed to crumble
Or find the quiet contemplation
Of a museum's memory.

Marking Time

James McGonigal

This poem is based on the five altar stones of Marcus Cocceius Firmus, centurion of the Second Augustan Legion, uncovered at Auchendavy Farm near Kirkintilloch.

Surviving that first year,
gladly I fulfilled my vow:
To Silvanus, god of fields and woods
who fed and warmed me.

For the second year's good hunting,
having learned to read the forest floor:
To Diana and Apollo deservedly
for both, this altar.

A third year come and gone:
In praise of Jupiter and Victory
my new altar stands here
unbeaten.

Fourth year. Under attack
I vowed: To Mars, Minerva and Epona
the horse goddess, to Hercules and all who bless
the ground where soldiers strive.

Latest and final season: To the spirit
of the land of Britain, whose mists
and green leaves covered me –
this stone's inscription.

*

From a hive near the bath house wall,
      clover honey and elderflower.

For incense to seek out heaven,
      beech charcoal or sycamore.

On sandstone hollowed smooth
as the heron mere

after rain when the bright arc is flung
like a tunic off the hill's shoulder –

what we offer today is given
      willingly and in duty.

*

Bleak watch at dawn. Slate-grey all day.
Sunset drips its augury into night.
What will remain of us

when we march south?
Altars stained with honey and wine
washed clean by rain on rain.

Between two seas and savage fells
we break or bury
what we cannot carry.

*

Smoke from Caledonian fires
tickles the nostrils of their god of sleet.
Demi-gods bicker in every stream.
　　　Did you not hear them?

We honoured deities of the leather tent,
of parade ground, anvil, hardened blades –
but in truth heard little from them
　　　when the mists came down.

Sandstone altars from the Antonine Wall

Five: The Move

Jemima Blackburn, *Moving the Contents of the Old College Museum*, 1870

The Move from High Street to Gilmorehill (1870)

Lesley Duncan

The celebrated Victorian artist Jemima Blackburn sketches the flitting
of The Hunterian animals, catching a pivotal moment in The Hunterian
Collection's history.

Jemima was her Christian name,
Inevitably provoking coupling with Puddleduck.
This levity would no doubt have amused
The real Jemima, married name Blackburn,
Wife of the Regius Professor of Mathematics
At Glasgow University, a marvellously talented artist
Whose close and often humorous observation
Of nature and animals is not dissimilar to that of Beatrix Potter
(Who was, incidentally, along with Ruskin and Landseer, an admirer).

One watercolour, particularly relevant to its times,
Shows the flitting of the Hunterian's stuffed animals
From their original home in Glasgow's High Street
To Gilbert Scott's mock-Gothic palace on Gilmorehill.
How graphically Jemima catches the removal scene!

An open cart provides the animals' transport.
On it, a polar bear, giant rump turned to viewers,
Has a slightly puzzled air, as well he might.
A lean tiger bares his teeth, partially obscuring a leopard.
A bearded gent with top hat, for all the world
Like a circus ringmaster, concentrates his attention

On mysterious striped animals with giant tails
(Could they be Caledonian diplodocuses?).
A forlorn giraffe is dragged on board by a hidden minion.

The hint of trees beyond the pillared background,
Serves as reminder of the vanished Dear Green Place.
Meanwhile, oblivious to his unusual cargo,
The waiting carthorse has his nose stuck in a feed-bag.
.
In the left foreground, the bonneted figure,
Sketchbook in hand, is Jemima herself.
What did she make of it all, one wonders?
Was she simply animated by artistic objectivity?
Did she share the prevailing Victorian arrogance
That all change was for the better? Or did she know,
And lament, that the College buildings once vacated,
Would crassly be destroyed for a railway goods-yard,
With all the imponderable loss of historical continuity
And intellectual heritage that that entailed?

Six:
Modernity

Andrew and the Hands
(at The Hunterian)

Jane Goldman

i'm stepping in from sunlight hurrying past so as not to inspect again
        too closely the gravid
uterus and those wooden forceps and the never unwrapped so in
        excellent condition body of Lady
Shep-en-hor's mummy past principles of beauty past horned
        screamer past shark's tooth (and this
is one of those teeth) past birds' nests in mid-nidification past phases
        of other animals' architecture when
the hands

arrest me
(oddly all three gleam) in a tender buttery nip this trio of polished
        wooden prosthetics produced by craftsmen
employed by the Yarrow Company Pattern shop in Glasgow as
        patterns to allow (as a matter of fact) disabled service
men and women at the Erskine Hospital to manufacture artificial
        limbs for the casualties returning from service
in World War One already melancholy they stir up the queerest of
        steers to me to hurry on past the opaque

Mona Lisa in Salon Six of the Louvre past all else of its pleasures in the
        louche Uffizi too a steer my friend Andrew first gave me
in '77 (so perfect he is texting me right now to say what we always
        silently knew that he prefers boys): go to the hands of the
        Titians
the ungloved saturnine index of the young sexy Man with a Glove
        points downward unwarring into the depths of a peaceful

earth the satyr discovers
himself cuckolded by the sleepy Venus del Pardo's own earthy hand
she is singing with wide-eyed Venus d'Urbino with Nicki
Minaj and Beyoncé too
i'm feeling myself

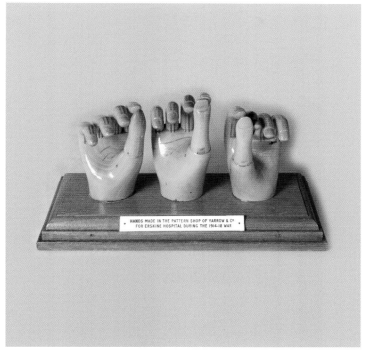

Early example of prosthetic hands made in the pattern shop at Yarrow and
Co. for Erskine Hospital, 1914-18

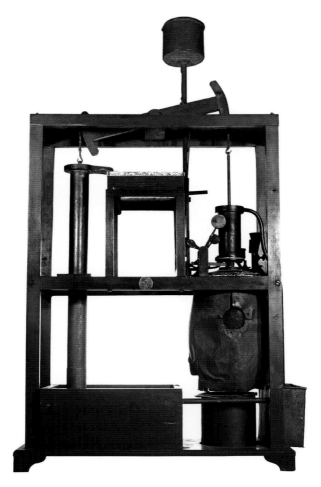

Model Newcomen steam engine, 18th century

Spending Time with Model Newcomen Steam Engine

Jim Carruth

The young instrument maker is left alone
with the task of repairing this small model.
Full scale it pumps water out of coal mines
allowing the men to dig deeper underground.

He is well aware how steam from a small boiler
should escape to fill the cylinder above it,
where a piston shifts the linked arch head
of the pivoting beam and lowers the pump rod.

From there cold water injected into the cylinder
will condense the steam creating a partial vacuum.
The greater pressure outside the cylinder
pushes the piston down, lifting the pump rod up.

He revels in the intricate detail of the process
but as a witness to its inefficient beauty
he questions the inevitable loss, the cooling.
This model after all is about the learning.

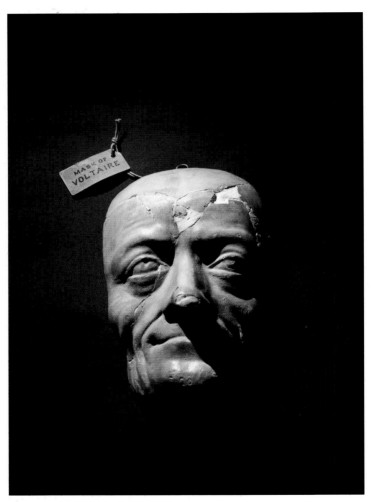

Death mask of Voltaire (1694-1778)

On the Nature and Propagation of Fire

John Glenday

'Chemistry informs us that fire is not an element, but a state through which bodies are passing.'

I always was the better one with numbers,
you, *mon petit volontaire*, with poetry, perhaps;

famous for words and so much more. I, only
for loving you. Those days, women thrived best

in shadow or part shade. I didn't seem to mind.
You said you adored my eyes – hazelly/green

like copper bound with iron, brightened in a flame -
the flame you couldn't forget, couldn't quite classify,

the flame you couldn't balance, couldn't weigh,
the flame you were given in a dream but couldn't

gather in your hands, then woke to the usual darkness
calling out my name. My love, I was that flame.

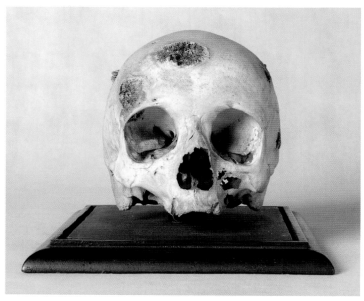

Example of a diseased skull from Hunter's pathological collection

Spirochaete

Pàdraig MacAoidh

Tha e doirbh a' cur an cèill
a' bhrisgeid seo, mar bhlàth choireil
neo groim a' bòrcadh air creagan,
briseach ach seasmhach,
a' sgròbadh tro chraiceann a' chinn

mar nàdar de dh'iongantas
a bheireas gu saoghal ùr thu
air gailleon reubte le rag-gèiltean,
na crainn do dhuilleógaibh dreasa
's na siùil mar nèapaigean robach

a' smèideadh, a' sìor smèideadh
mar a tha nàire a' sìor fhàs
fo shùil bheachdaidh Dhè,
a luchd-glèidhidh 's a mhaoir-chìse,
mar shlige-neamhnaid a' snìomhadh a bhith.

Tha dòigh aig eachdraidh. Tha caran ann.
Mar a bha fios aig Fracastro,
seo mar a tha meatafor a' fàs,
a' càrnadh, a' tarmachadh,
air bhleith agus air ithe le leòmannan,

mar dhìleab thairis air do dh'fhulangais,
ged a dh' fhàs e unnad, a' lagachadh
na th'unnad, agus fiù's do chlaban
a' fàs a bhìth na drùis, na làthach,
pleataichean-rùisg a' sgiorradh thar na boglaich.

Feuchaidh tu guaiacum, airgead-beò, salvarsan,
ach fàsaidh e bhith tuilleadh 's doirbh
a chur an cèill gur ann mar seo a tha caochladh
a' faireachdainn: biorgadh 's crith;
leigeil leis, leigeil às.

Ruith bas do làimhe thar an sgarpa bhreacaich.
Thèid trup eile dhan a' bheàirn.

Spirochaete
Peter Mackay

It is hard to imagine this fragility,
like a bloom of coral or polyp
budding on rocks,
anfractuous but resolute,
scraping through the scalp

like the kind of curiosity that takes you
to a new world on a gale-torn galleon,
its masts made of bramble-leaves
and its sails ragged handkerchiefs
waving, forever waving

as shame will always grow
under the attentive eye of God
his guardians and taxmen,
like nacre spiralling into being.
History has a way. There are twists.

As Fracastro understood, this is how
metaphor grows, through accretion
and accumulation, through erosion,
being eaten by moths,
as a legacy beyond your endurance

even though it grew in you,
as it weakens what you are ,
as your skull becomes an ooze,
a sludge, plates of crust
sliding over a bog.

You might try guaiacum,
mercury, salvarsan,
but it will become ever harder to imagine
that this is what change feels like:
twitch and quake, letting be, forgetting.

Run your palm gently along that pucked ridge.
Go once more unto the breach.

Duddingston Curling Society medal, 1806

The Curler's Coort
Sheena Blackhall

Initiation: **The** *Word and the Grip*

In order to prevent all disputes concerning the curler word and grip, the master, who always is present during his office, and the rest of the society, have agreed that the following shall be held and reputed the curler word and grip of this society for the future:
The curler word:

If you'd be a curler keen
Stand right, look even,
Sole well, shoot straight, and sweep clean.

The curler grip, with the explanation:
'The curler is initiated by receiving the grip, which consists in catching him by the thumb in the manner that the curling-stone is held, and in making him repeat the curling word: 'I promise never to go to the ice without a broom; I will fit fair, sweep well, take all the brittle (angled) shots I can, and tangle (dispute) to a hair-breadth.'

The Belfast Club at their annual meetings had much 'exhilarating and side-splitting mirth' under the court. On one occasion (January 9, 1880) a live donkey, which had, unknown to most of the members, been placed in a large press in the banqueting-hall, gave a loud bray in the middle of an eloquent speech by the chaplain Rev. W.C. M'Cullagh), and 'brought down the house.' The 'noble steed' was afterwards trotted out, and each candidate for initiation had to approach 'My Lord' on the donkey's back, with his face to the tail and a broom kowe over his right shoulder. *Dulce est desipere in loco.* 'Weel-timed daffin' is very enjoyable, and the quaint custom of the curling court may have a place among the diversions that help

To cheer us through the weary widdle
O' wai'ly cares.

The Abdie Club, under the licence of the court, actually made up the most of its funds by court fines of the most hanky-panky description, inflicted on all and sundry without rhyme or reason. We give a few specimens:

'February 1, 1841.— Dr L. was fined 1s. for shooting at a hare in her seat, the offence being aggravated by the fact that the hare had been dead for some days previous.

'January 31, 1844.— Mr Russel, without consent of the club, having purchased an estate, was fined 2s. 6d.

'February 1859.— A.W.R., for having, to the great danger of the digestion and bodily health of the members present, supplied hard, tough beef for this day's dinner, was fined 1s.

'Mr Pitcairn, for being the first member of the club who had condescended to the use of chloroform in having a tooth extracted, was fined 2s. 6d.

Twa o my kin gaed throwe the Curler's Coort
Their lips wir steekit on the ongauns there
It wis weel-kent a rowth o drink wis taen
Bi aa involved in thon high-jinks affair

I've heard it said a goat wis mangst the thrang
An whyles a brukken neb or shank or airm
In Coorts langsyne, fin things gaed ooto haun
Itherwise, nae ill-meant wi little herm

A grown-up plisky, secrets kittle up
The weary darg o kintra life an wyes
Licht-hairtit, as fin a fat brosie wife
Sat doon tae rest, rifts, an lats oot her steys

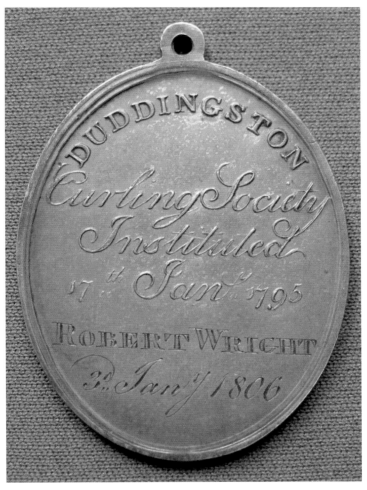

Duddingston Curling Society medal, 1806

Sir Hubert von Herkomer, *Lord Kelvin*, 1891

One Proof for Lord Kelvin's Second Law of Thermodynamics

Jim Carruth

Heat will not flow from a colder body to a hotter body
Heat will not flow from an older body to a hotter toddy
Heat will not flow from a gaudy folder to a shoddy jotter
Heat will not flow from a modern moulder to an orthodox potter
Heat will not flow from a smallish smoulder to a Guy Fawkes plotter
Heat will not flow from a proud householder to a soapbox squatter
Heat will not flow from a rich shareholder to a foreign slaughter
Heat will not flow from your cold shoulder
Heat will not flow from you
Heat will not know you
Heat will not glow
Heat will slow
Heat will go
Heat will
Go cold
In you

Taxidermy mount of a neonate fallow deer, *Dama dama*, showing
developmental defect known in 19th century as 'dicephalus tetrabrachius'

Untitled
Gerry Cambridge

It could be a matter for terror, this
place of medical instrument
and elegant dissection,
factually labelled;
some minute coding error made
the four front legs, twin heads,
facing each other as if they fought,
of the little fallow deer
standing up, bipedal, like a man...
And the whole
fabulous, detailed world of light
at a stroke
gone black

Some far
personal catastrophe
one ordinary day or night
explained by a burst aorta, white
now as tissue paper
anonymous, in a specimen jar

Lord Kelvin's artificial pitch glacier, 1887

GLAHM 113597

John Purser

There is nothing more peaceful
than this silent experiment
a mahogany ramp
a lump of pitch
stretching itself
with almost infinite luxury
down the slope.

They say it's glacial
but glaciers break up, advance, retreat
almost as rapidly as armies
in a continental war.

Not so this staircase of
imperceptible pitch
sliding from note to note
down the scalar descent
gravitas gravitatum et omnia gravitas.

Pitch black from top
to bottom 'cobbler's wax'
shattering like glass
under the hammer blow
but here
sliding ominously slow
like a sleepy snake

There is nothing more peaceful
than this silent experiment
yet it was designed to produce
turbulence.

Somewhere in Lord Kelvin's mind
the aether had form and substance
of a kind, and space was filled
with the currents of viscous tides.

The aether has vanished. How?
Into the aether. That's where aether goes.
But this inexorable flow
of darkness
challenges the darkness of our minds.

Solid or liquid, this calcified oil
could be as fractious
as shards of coal at the coalface,
as slippy and silent as honey
on a tiled floor.

And as for that turbulence
there is nothing so quiet
no experiment so secluded
no thought so protected
that it cannot be disturbed
by the insistences of life

the necessity of motion to matter.

'all matter duly formed is attended with signs of life.'

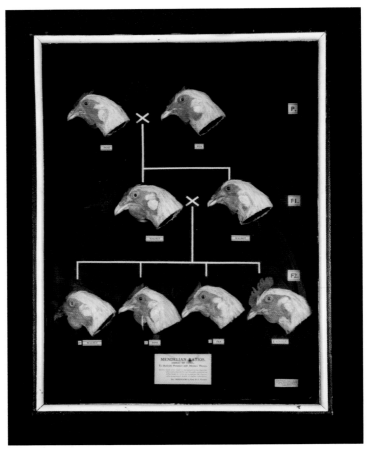

Box of taxidermied domestic chicken (*Gallus domesticus*) heads to show variation in the comb form. Illustrates a basic principle of classic genetics - the di-hybrid cross.

Heads Up
(a display explaining Mendelian inheritance)
Jim Carruth

In retrospect of course it makes sense
with all the talk of headless chickens

What ever happpened to their heads?
Well some of them are presented here

in this dusty old wooden specimen case.
I'm not sure the right collective noun

without wings they are hardly a flock
a hutch of heads? a clutch of heads?

Laid out on perches, linked by lines
a pecking order of sorts at play here.

That mad Augustan monk, Gregor Mendel
would've understood more fully the clues

that hang in the shape of their red combs
ratios of single, walnut, pea and rose.

Sorry children you can't avoid inheritance
though an ingredient might skip a generation.

With genetics the key, every day you can meet
the living ancestors in your own offspring.

I try to make connections from the evidence:

echoes of the dead across corn-fed generations;

while the related heads in front of me,
nod and wink knowingly to each other.

Plaster cast of the gravid uterus at full term

Delivery
Richie McCaffery

'One of the young men seized the rope and pulled by it, but the old
enchantment of the devil remained, – it would not break.'
James Hogg, *The Private Memoirs and Confessions of a Justified Sinner*

Midwives all, the men and women
traipsing through The Hunterian,
who see a glass jar full of alcohol
and drink in the shock of a motherless
Georgian uterus and foetus.

I see that child born and adopted
or disowned by those who look at it,
their eyes reaching in and pulling
only to find the umbilical cord
still strong, tethered to nothing.

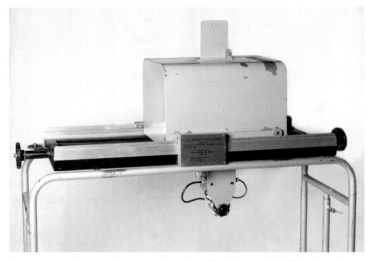

A prototype ultrasound scanner developed in Glasgow for clinical use in gynaecology and obstetrics © CSG CIC Glasgow Museums Collection

First Experimental Contact B-Scanner British Patent no. 863.874

Peter McCarey

The youngest foreman plater on the Clyde
When his youngest (my father) was three, fell to pneumonia
That I, at three, survived to see
Pickled freak friends in this curious
Cabinet, fossil bones and Roman coins but not
Till now the chest for checking
Welds at my father's work, rejigged
To scry cockle mariners such as
My daughter, scanned at the Southern,
Now expert in its use,
Every bit of this Hunterian,
Steam Gothic tor in time
The shade of a sound.

Seven:
The Hunterian Collection

Allan Ramsay, *William Hunter*, 1764-65

The Curiosities of Dr Hunter
Gerrie Fellows

Dr Hunter's cabinet of marvels
polished to a high gloss
frames the body parts of beauties
a nymph

dry-pinned
the sheen of a carapace
the startling sash of brilliant wings
fixed under mirroring glass

Neptune beetle   made up of parts
head and thorax of a true Scarab
staked to paper
a recipe for a fake

or an invention
for the naturally curious to unravel

as Lady St Aubyn's gift
of Cornish ores
(the raw core of tin mines)
was an invitation to know the ground

the mineral heart of his collection
six hundred jaspers   agates
translucent as insect wings
lucid amber   traders' gems

quartz in a chert concretion
one of Pocock's petrified melons
delicious but inedible
case of mistaken identity

and identification
was the name of the game
God's perfect arrangements
thrown into doubt

by the fossil sequence
unearthed
from coal measures or limestone
Cuvier's proof of extinction

Corals   insects   shells
the wealth
of Dr Fothergill's collection
a purchase on nature's profusion

the Endeavour's prize   flower
and artifice of southern oceans
the materia of a living culture
or relics for an age of wonder?

for his antiquarium   a case
of the long-gone swaddled dead
(grave good was to come of it
and did)

all manner of curiosities
even Linnaeus
original of the collecting mind
preserved here   a bronze medal

beside the image of fortune
a mother with her sun king
embraced in a silver roundel
bulbed as a pregnant womb

The core of the matter
in the doctor's mind
(before the Rembrandts
the Hogarth engravings)

manuscripts   incunabula
historical medical treatises
books as hooks to hang his thinking on
anatomical samples

wet specimens and dry bones
diseased and intricate as coral
the bony eminence
of a skull deformed

the anatomy of the human
gravid uterus
ravaged yet no grave goods
for his cabinet of curiosities

(though the book's a cabinet too)

a woman   nine months pregnant
cut open in secret
revealed in cross section
on the page's two dimensions

a natural object   unidentified
(habitat London   Camberwell Beauty?)

her death   an instruction
for science   and the safety of royals

Jars   drawers   trays of glass
wood sheened to high gloss
to polish off the stain of rumour
a shimmer

as if the body of knowledge
were exposed   flayed to muscle

the man of natural curiosities
(up-and-coming anatomist
obstetrician to royalty)
makes his own entrance

in history   (reputation intact)
a man of science   winging it
among butterflies and body parts
and his own death mask .